# Dropshipping shopify for Amateurs 2024

The Complete Dropshipping Shopify Handbook that provides a comprehensive guide to building a successful dropshipping business from launch to long-term success.

Anna P. Moore

# Table of contents

# Chapter One

**Understanding the business model and the potential of dropshipping**

### *1.1. What exactly is dropshipping?*

The first part of the chapter provides a definition of dropshipping, which is a technique of retail fulfilment in which you, as the proprietor of the shop, do not physically possess the merchandise that you sell. On the other hand, when a consumer puts an order in your online shop, you take on the role of a middleman and send the purchase details and customer information to a third-party provider. After that, this provider will package the goods and dispatch them straight to your client, after which they will handle all of the logistics associated with storage, fulfilment, and shipping.

## 1.2 *The advantages of drop shipping are as follows:*

The next section of the chapter digs into the primary benefits of dropshipping, which are the reasons why it is an appealing choice for many ambitious business owners, particularly those who are just starting out in the field of e-commerce:

*Low Initial Investment Required:* There is very little initial investment necessary, which is one of the most appealing aspects of dropshipping. When it comes to acquiring merchandise, hiring warehouse space, or handling shipping logistics, you do not need to spend a lot on these activities. This enables you to establish your company with less risk and test alternative goods without substantial financial investment.

*Scalability:* Dropshipping has significant scaling possibilities. As your firm expands, you don't have to worry about handling more inventory or fulfilling orders yourself. Your suppliers manage the growth in demand, enabling you to develop your firm effectively and concentrate on marketing and customer service.

*Wide Product Range:* Unlike typical retail establishments constrained by physical area, dropshipping enables you to provide a large assortment of items. You may simply add or delete goods from your shop based on market trends and client preferences, offering you additional flexibility and agility.

*Location Independence:* The brilliance of dropshipping rests in its geographical freedom. You may operate your company from anywhere on the globe with an internet connection, enabling more flexibility and lifestyle freedom.

## *1.3. Understanding the Dropshipping Landscape:*

The chapter doesn't shy away from offering a realistic picture of the dropshipping landscape. It explains the many actors engaged in the process, including:

*Dropshippers:* You, the shop owner, operate the online store and handle the customer-facing portions of the business.

*Suppliers:* These third-party firms maintain the inventory, package, and ship the items straight to your consumers. *

*Customers:* As the lifeblood of every company, you cater to their demands by offering a user-friendly online shop and exceptional customer service.

### 1.4. The Importance of Market Research and Niche Selection:

The chapter underlines the need for rigorous market research in dropshipping. It illustrates how establishing a successful niche market is vital for success. Focusing on a particular target demographic with distinct requirements and preferences helps you adjust your product offering, marketing techniques, and overall brand identity to connect with them successfully.

**_1.5. Potential Challenges and Considerations:_** No company strategy is without its hurdles, and dropshipping is no exception. The chapter highlights certain limitations you'll need to be aware of and manage effectively:

*smaller profit margins:* Due to the participation of many parties, the profit margins in dropshipping tend to be smaller compared to typical retail models. This demands effective marketing techniques and increased sales volume to achieve profitability.

*Competition:* The dropshipping space is getting extremely competitive. The chapter underscores the necessity of distinguishing your company through unique product offers, outstanding customer service, and successful marketing techniques.

*Limited Control over Fulfilment:* Since you depend on third-party providers for fulfilment, you have less control over product quality, delivery delays, and the overall customer experience. Finding competent and trustworthy providers with a solid track record is vital to reducing these risks.

### 1.6. Is Dropshipping Right for You?

The chapter finishes by helping you through some self-reflection questions to examine if dropshipping corresponds with your aims and ambitions. It underlines the significance of examining your risk tolerance, available resources, and commitment level before commencing on this entrepreneurial adventure.

By knowing the principles of dropshipping, studying its advantages and limitations, and completing comprehensive market research, you'll be well-equipped to make an educated conclusion about whether this business model is the best match for you. This thorough introduction prepares you for the following chapter, which goes further into the dropshipping order fulfilment process, setting the framework for developing your successful e-commerce company.

Shopify stands as one of several options for creating an online store, yet it has become the go-to choice for many entrepreneurs venturing into e-commerce.

## Understanding Shopify and Its Benefits for Dropshipping

Shopify is a user-friendly platform that enables individuals to establish an online store without the need for programming skills. It is cost-effective and offers extensive customization to achieve the desired aesthetic for your site. Here are key reasons why Shopify is a top selection for dropshipping:

*1. Versatility of Shopify*
Shopify boasts remarkable versatility, allowing for easy customization of your website. With a simple interface, you can:

- Introduce product categories
- Craft blog entries
- Add new pages
- Modify sections
- Incorporate hero banners or video segments

The platform grants you the freedom to differentiate your store, regardless of your chosen theme.

*2. Cost-effectiveness of Shopify*
As of the latest update, Shopify's monthly fee is $29, granting you access to a fully operational dropshipping store with unlimited product uploads. This plan also includes:

- Additional sales channels like Facebook
- Coupon code generation
- An SSL certificate for your site
- Marketing automation tools
- Integration capabilities with other platforms
- Automated shipping options and pricing

Moreover, the Basic Plan supports various payment gateways, including Stripe and PayPal, simplifying the process of online transactions.

*3. Abundance of Shopify Apps*

Shopify's app marketplace houses thousands of apps to enhance your store's functionality and design, such as:

- Promotional apps for deals like buy-one-get-one offers
- Email marketing tools
- Apps for product reviews with image or video uploads

While Shopify offers a multitude of apps, it's advisable for newcomers to dropshipping to initially focus on the free options before investing in paid subscriptions.

Despite the presence of alternative platforms like WooCommerce, BigCommerce, Ecwid, Squarespace, and others, Shopify remains a preferred choice due to its simplicity and speed in setting up a dropshipping store.

### How Shopify Functions

You'll construct an online store using Shopify, where you can upload product details, images, and set shipping rates. This process can be automated with various apps that facilitate product imports and other necessary details into your Shopify store.

### *The Profitability of Shopify Dropshipping*

Dropshipping with Shopify can be quite profitable with minimal overhead costs, primarily the $29 monthly subscription. For example, selling a t-shirt acquired for $9.95 from the supplier at $29.95 in your store yields a $20 profit per shirt. Selling 50 shirts a month would result in a gross profit of $1,000. After deducting the subscription fee, the net profit stands at $975.

Even if sales are slow initially, the low monthly expense makes it a manageable risk, especially compared to daily discretionary spending like coffee purchases.

### *Steps to Begin Dropshipping with Shopify*
To establish your Shopify dropshipping business, follow these high-level steps:

1. Establish a Brand Identity and Niche
First, determine your brand identity and select a niche market. This involves:

- Securing a domain name
- Creating a logo
- Designing a favicon

Your domain should reflect your business name and be memorable. Once acquired, integrate it with your Shopify store and either hire a designer or use online tools for your logo and favicon.

*2. Set Up Your Shopify Store*
Register for a Shopify account and opt for the Basic
Plan. Important initial settings include:

- Setting your store's currency
- Creating product collections
- Enabling gift cards
- Configuring payment gateways and sales channels
- Inputting business details

Explore all settings thoroughly to tailor your store to your
needs.

*3. Create Essential Pages*
Develop standard pages for your website, such as:

- About Us
- Terms & Conditions
- Shipping and Refund Policy
- Privacy Policy

Templates are available online for these documents;
customize them to suit your business.

*4. Customize Your Theme*
Choose from free or paid themes on Shopify and
customize your chosen theme to align with your brand's
style guide, which includes color schemes, fonts, and
other branding elements.

*5. Install Apps*

Enhance your store with apps from Shopify's marketplace, focusing on those that offer the most value. Stick with free apps initially to keep costs down.

In summary, while Shopify is among many e-commerce platforms, its ease of use, affordability, and extensive app ecosystem make it an attractive choice for entrepreneurs, particularly in the realm of dropshipping.

*Consider incorporating the following essential app categories:*

- A product importing tool, such as Spocket.
- A product research tool, like Dropship.IO.
- Apps for offering discounts and coupons.
- Apps for product bundles or buy-one-get-one promotions.
- Email marketing applications.
- Apps that provide social proof.
- Abandoned cart recovery applications.

Initially, prioritize marketing-related apps, as they play a crucial role in generating sales and conversions for your store. However, be cautious not to overload your store with too many apps, as this can significantly slow down your website's performance.

*6. Importing Products to Your Store*

When you're ready to add products to your store, consider the following steps:

- Standardize the presentation of your products.
- Configure price automation in Shopify, deciding whether to add a flat rate or a percentage markup to all products.
- Identify products that may need improved images or descriptions.

After importing, categorize your products into collections, such as placing all leather shoes in a "Leather Shoes" collection. You'll then need to manually edit product pages to ensure consistency across descriptions from different suppliers.

### 7. Launching and Marketing Your Shopify Dropshipping Store

Before launching your store, conduct a test purchase to ensure everything functions correctly. Log out of your Shopify account and make a purchase as a customer would. Order the product from your supplier and have it shipped to your address to experience the full customer journey and identify any issues.

Once everything is verified, you can focus on creating social media content and planning your posting schedule. With a solid marketing strategy in place, you're ready to start your business.

### *Choosing a Winning Product for Dropshipping*

Selecting a successful dropshipping product requires careful consideration. Here's what to look for:

1. Market Demand: Verify the product's sales volume to gauge interest and demand.

2. Product Quality: Ensure the product's quality justifies your selling price.

3. Shipping Details: Assess the supplier's shipping speed, international coverage, and costs.

4. Market Competition: Use tools to check how many other dropshippers are selling the same product.

### *Marketing Your Shopify Dropshipping Store*

There are three primary marketing strategies for your Shopify store:

- Blogging and SEO: Use Shopify's blogging feature to publish informative articles and improve your SEO.
- SEM and Advertising: Pay for search engine ads to appear at the top of search results for specific keywords.
- Social Media Posting: Regularly post content on social media platforms to engage with your audience.

Choose the marketing approach that aligns with your budget and expertise to effectively promote your store.

### *Search Engine Marketing (SEM) & Advertising*

SEM is a specialized form of advertising that is limited to search engines. Consider the following example:

When searching for "drone for sale in the United States" on Google, the first listing that appears is a paid advertisement by Aquidneck Aerials, indicating that they have invested in their visibility for this specific search term.

The result is that users, including myself, might click on this prominent ad, leading us to the advertiser's landing page. However, upon closer inspection, it becomes clear that the company doesn't sell drones but rather offers aerial photography services. This illustrates a misalignment between keyword targeting and actual service offerings, which is an inefficient use of advertising resources. It is crucial to align your Google advertising efforts with keywords that accurately reflect your business offerings.

When it comes to advertising on social media, the platform selection should be strategic, based on where potential customers for your product are most active:

- Instagram is optimal for products like lipstick, makeup, and health and beauty items.
- TikTok is suitable for entertainment, games, and hobby-related content.

- Facebook is versatile and can accommodate a wide range of products.

Remember, advertising requires investment. I once spent $1,000 without a return, so it's important to proceed carefully, learn effective advertising strategies, and incrementally increase your spending.

### *Social Media Marketing*

Marketing your products on social media can be done through regular posting, akin to blogging but on social platforms. Choose the right platform based on your product category, and focus on sharing insightful, educational, or entertaining content rather than overt marketing messages.

For instance, showcase your drone in action through a video that highlights the experience and fun it can provide, rather than just listing its features. Content that entertains and engages emotionally is more likely to generate interaction and lead to sales.

### *Dropshipping on Shopify and Other Platforms*

Dropshipping with AliExpress requires the use of a tool that connects you with suppliers on the platform. Spocket and CJDropshipping are two recommended options.

For beginners looking to dropship on Shopify, it's advisable to watch comprehensive tutorials on setting up a Shopify store. You can also consider purchasing a pre-built store.

Dropshipping on Shopify isn't free; after a 7-day trial, you'll need to choose a subscription plan.

To dropship on Amazon, integrate your Shopify store with your Amazon seller account, or use a tool like Spocket directly with Amazon.

Dropshipping on Shopify without initial funds isn't feasible; expect to invest a minimum monthly fee.

For those interested in dropshipping with Alibaba, which is primarily a wholesale platform, you can coordinate with CJDropshipping to connect with Alibaba suppliers for your Shopify store.

To start dropshipping on Shopify, identify products to sell from platforms compatible with Shopify, create your store, and import your chosen products.

Is dropshipping on Shopify worthwhile? Absolutely, as the monthly investment is relatively low compared to the potential profits.

Shopify does support dropshipping and integrates with numerous supplier tools such as Spocket, Printful, Salehoo, Printify, and Dropified.

# Chapter Two

**The Dropshipping Order Fulfilment Process: From Customer Purchase to Delivery**

After covering the principles and possibilities of dropshipping in the previous chapter, this chapter digs into the subtle dance of the dropshipping order fulfilment process. It describes the path of an order, from the moment a consumer clicks "buy" on your online site until the time the goods arrive at their door.

***1.1. A Customer Places an Order:*** The process starts when a consumer visits your online shop, browses your product selection, adds an item to their basket, and proceeds to checkout. During this step, it is critical to provide a user-friendly and secure checkout experience to guarantee a seamless consumer journey.

***1.2. Order Processing and Forwarding:*** Following a successful order placement, your dropshipping company takes centre stage. You get an order notice with the customer's information and the exact product(s) purchased.

Here are your responsibilities:

A) Order Verification and Payment Processing: You validate the order data, assure payment security, and may undertake fraud checks as needed.

B) Order Forwarding to Supplier: This is where the essence of drop-shipping comes into play. You send the validated order information (including client information, product specifications, and delivery instructions) to your preferred supplier.

*1.3. Supplier Fulfilment:*Once the provider gets your order, they will conduct the following tasks:

A) Inventory Check:Ensures the requested item is in stock and ready for fulfilment.

B) Product Picking and Packing: Locate the product in the warehouse, carefully pick it, and securely pack it for safe shipment.

C) Order Labelling and Shipping:They apply the proper shipping label, including the customer's address and any relevant customs papers (for foreign orders), then ship the product via their preferred shipping carrier.

***1.4. Order Tracking and Communication with Customers:***While the supplier handles actual fulfilment, you, as the dropshipper, play an important role in keeping the consumer informed.

*Order Confirmation and Tracking Details:* You send the client an email confirming their purchase, giving the projected delivery period and a tracking number (given by the supplier) so they may check their package's progress.

*Customer service:* You serve as the customer's principal point of contact throughout the process.

You respond to any questions or concerns they have about their order, shipping status, or possible complications.

### *1.5. Delivery and After-Purchase Experience:*
The last step includes delivering the product to the consumer. Once the delivery is delivered, the customer's experience is essential.

As a drop-shipper, you should consider the following:

A) Delivery Confirmation: To guarantee that the consumer receives their purchase, send them a notice verifying delivery.

B) Customer Reviews and Feedback: Encourage customers to submit reviews on your website or preferred channel. This feedback is helpful in strengthening your store's reputation and recruiting new consumers.

***1.6. Manage Returns and Refunds:*** Even with the greatest preparation, unexpected events like product damage, wrong shipments, or customer discontent may result in returns. The chapter examines how to deal with such circumstances effectively.

*Clear Return Policy:* Having a clearly stated return policy on your website establishes expectations and simplifies the process for both you and the client.

*Return Communication:* Create a clear communication method for consumers to request returns and obtain reimbursements.

*Collaboration with Supplier:* Depending on the conditions of your agreement, you may collaborate with your supplier to handle the return and refund process, providing a seamless and satisfying experience for the consumer.

Understanding and mastering the dropshipping order fulfilment process allows you to provide a smooth and good experience for your consumers, creating trust and loyalty, which are critical components of developing a successful e-commerce company. This chapter will provide you with the information you need to successfully handle this crucial component of your dropshipping journey.

## *Niche and Product Selection: Identifying Your Profitable Market Segment*

Success in dropshipping depends on selecting the correct niche and items. This chapter will help you through the process of discovering a successful market niche and choosing items that appeal to your target audience.

## *2.1. Recognising the Value of Niche Selection:*

The chapter opens by emphasising the importance of niche selection in dropshipping. Choosing a specialised specialty enables you to:

*Target a Specific Audience:* By catering to a well-defined client group with distinct wants and preferences, you may better align your product offers, marketing techniques, and overall brand identity.

*Reduce Competition:* Instead of competing in a crowded market with several established brands, concentrating on a niche helps you to stand out and even position yourself as a leader in your chosen sector.

*Increase Expertise and Brand Authority:* Focusing on a certain specialty helps you obtain a better grasp of your target market's demands and preferences. This enables you to establish yourself as an expert in your field, allowing you to gain the confidence and authority of your consumers.

## 2.2. Identifying Profitable Niches:

The chapter provides you with useful ideas and tactics for identifying potentially profitable niches:

**Market Research and Trend Analysis:** Use internet tools, social media platforms, and industry journals to find new trends, client wants, and popular product categories. Observing how established brands in other areas operate may also provide useful information.

**Identifying Your Passions and Skills:** Reflect on your own interests, hobbies, and areas of competence. Choosing a specialisation that you are enthusiastic about can help you remain motivated and involved in the long term. Furthermore, using your current talents and experience might create a competitive advantage in that area.

**Evaluating Niche Profitability:** Do not base your decision only on a niche's popularity. Competition, product margins, and client acquisition expenses are all important considerations for assessing profitability. Before reducing your focus, use internet tools and resources to examine the potential profitability of the niches you've identified.

## 2.3. Define Your Target Audience:

Once you've discovered a prospective niche, this chapter will walk you through the process of identifying your target audience.

**Demographics:** Use age, gender, geography, economic level, and employment to build a clear image of your ideal consumer.
**Psychographics:** Explore your target audience's interests, hobbies, beliefs, and pain areas to better understand their motivations and requirements. Understanding their "why" enables you to create engaging marketing messages that connect with them.

## *2.4. Choose Winning Products:*

Now comes the interesting part: deciding which things to offer inside your selected niche. The chapter gives you a path for making educated product selection choices.

I) *Problem-solving items:* Look for items that solve particular issues or obstacles experienced by your target audience. Focusing on solutions rather than features helps you build a relationship with your clients.

II) *Profit Margin Analysis:* Determine the possible profit margin for each product, taking into consideration the selling price, supplier costs, and other related expenditures. To secure the long-term viability of your firm, choose items with a solid profit margin.

III) *Market Demand and Competition:* Determine the degree of market demand and competition for the items you're thinking about. While good competition indicates a flourishing specialty, too much rivalry might make it tough to distinguish.

*IV) Product Trends and Seasonality:* Think about current market trends and the probable seasonality of the items you pick. Riding the wave of trends may increase sales, but be wary of potentially short-lived fads.

V) *Supplier Quality and Reliability:Aqa*Conduct due diligence on possible suppliers, evaluating their product quality, delivery timeframes, customer service reputation, and minimum order quantities (MOQs) to guarantee a smooth and dependable experience.

## 2.5. Creating a Cohesive Product Portfolio

The chapter focuses not just on individual items, but also on the significance of developing a unified product portfolio within your selected niche.

**Complementary goods:** Provide goods that compliment one another, encouraging clients to buy more things and increasing their average order value.

**Curated Selection:** Avoid overwhelming your consumers with a too broad product offering. Instead, create a collection that meets the unique wants and interests of your target audience.

**Maintaining Brand Relevance:** Make sure your selected items match your overall brand identity and message, resulting in a consistent and recognisable experience for your consumers.

By mastering the art of niche and product selection, you set the framework for a successful dropshipping venture. This chapter provides you with the information and tactics you need to find lucrative niches, define your target audience, and choose winning items that will connect with your consumers and contribute to the long-term success of your dropshipping company.

# Chapter Three

**Identifying the Ideal Dropshipping Vendors: Forming Robust Collaborations.**

For your dropshipping company to succeed, you must build solid relationships with dependable and trustworthy suppliers. This chapter explores the process of identifying the ideal dropshipping providers, setting the groundwork for a seamless and effective fulfilment procedure that will eventually result in satisfied clients and a flourishing company.

*1.1. Selecting the Correct Suppliers Is Crucial:* The first point of the chapter is to emphasise how important suppliers are to your dropshipping operation. They serve as the foundation of your fulfilment process and have a direct influence on things like:

 **Product Quality:** Your clients depend on you to provide them with top-notch goods. Reliability and quality control are prioritised by reputable suppliers, which guarantees customer happiness and lowers the possibility of returns and bad reviews.

*Reliability and Speed of Shipping:* For customers to be satisfied, deliveries must be made on time. Your clients will get their goods on time if you choose providers with dependable shipping partners and effective shipping procedures.

*Customer Service:* Although you, the dropshipper, are your clients' first point of contact, the quality of service provided by your supplier may affect the whole experience. Associating with vendors renowned for their superior customer service guarantees that any problems are resolved quickly and effectively.

*Price and Profit Margins:* Your profit margins are directly impacted by the amount you pay your supplier. Maintaining healthy profit margins in your dropshipping company requires negotiating competitive rates and taking into account particulars like minimum order quantities (MOQs).

**1.2. *Locating Possible Dropshipping Providers:*** This chapter gives you a number of tools to find possible dropshipping suppliers:

***internet directories:*** Dropshipping providers are listed and categorised in a wide range of areas by several internet directories. Use these directories as a foundation for your investigation.

***Industry Research:*** Investigating well-known companies in the niche you've selected might expose their suppliers or provide hints about reliable suppliers in your field.

***Trade exhibitions and online marketplaces:*** You may meet possible dropshipping suppliers by going to trade exhibitions in the sector or by looking into online marketplaces like Alibaba or Sprocket.

**Social Media and Online Reviews:** Reach out to other dropshippers on social media sites like Facebook groups or LinkedIn to get their suggestions for trustworthy suppliers.

**1.3. *Assessing Suppliers Who Dropship:*** Following the identification of possible suppliers, the chapter walks you through a rigorous assessment process to make sure they meet your requirements as a business:

**Product Quality and Range:** Evaluate the supplier's offerings to make sure the quality meets your brand's requirements as well as those of your customers. Examine the range of items available to see if they align with the product portfolio you have in mind.

**Shipping Rates and Delivery Times:** Examine the expected delivery times and shipping costs provided by various vendors. For you to stay competitive and provide your clients with realistic shipping expectations, this information is essential.

**Ordinance Minimums (MOQs):** Take note of the minimum order quantities (MOQs) that each supplier has established. These may affect how you manage your inventory and cash flow, particularly if you're beginning with a tight budget.* Payment conditions and return policies: Recognise the supplier's payment conditions, including deadlines and modes of payment.

Check their return policies as well to make sure they are clear and kind to customers.

**Customer Service Support:** Assess the prospective supplier's level of customer service excellence. This may be accomplished by speaking with them directly, looking up internet evaluations, or seeing how quickly they respond to inquiries from customers.

**1.4. Establishing Robust Supplier Connections:** The chapter stresses the need to establish solid and long-lasting relationships with suppliers in addition to locating them. The following are some crucial tactics:

*Clear Communication and Expectations:* Create clear channels of communication and set expectations for order processing, product quality, and delivery schedules.

*Regular Communication and Collaboration:* Stay in constant contact with your suppliers to discuss possible problems in advance, look into new product opportunities, and build a cooperative relationship.

***Timely Payments and Order Updates:*** Make sure payments are made on time and give accurate order updates to keep your suppliers happy. You may find and work with trustworthy dropshipping suppliers that share your dedication to efficiency, quality, and customer pleasure by using the advice in this chapter.

Establishing robust and cooperative connections with your suppliers is crucial for guaranteeing the seamless functioning of your dropshipping business and laying the groundwork for sustained prosperity.

### *Building Your Dropshipping Business: Setting Up Your Dropshipping Store: Choosing the Right Platform and Design*

Your online shop serves as the virtual showroom for your dropshipping company, connecting you with possible clients and showcasing your product range. This chapter walks you through the critical steps of choosing the best platform and creating an aesthetically pleasing and easy-to-use shop that builds consumer confidence and motivates them to make purchases.

***Selecting the Appropriate Dropshipping Marketplace:***

The need of choosing the appropriate platform to create your dropshipping business is emphasised at the beginning of the chapter. There are many platforms available, each with unique features, disadvantages, and cost structures. When selecting your choice, keep the following important considerations in mind:

**Ease of Use:** To make the establishment and administration of your business easier if you're new to e-commerce, take into consideration platforms renowned for their intuitive features and user-friendly layout.
**Features and Functionality:** Consider the features that each platform provides, including built-in SEO functions, payment gateway

alternatives, marketing connectors, and product management tools. Select a platform based on what your company requirements are now and in the future.

**Pricing and Scalability:** Examine the various platforms' pricing schemes, taking into account both recurring fees and transaction expenses. Make sure the platform you choose can handle the expansion of your company and rising sales volumes as it grows.

**App Marketplace and Integrations:** Numerous systems enable interfaces with various external services, such as shipping companies, accounting software, and email marketing tools. Additionally, check to see whether the app markets on each platform have features and extensions that align with your company requirements.

**1.2. Well-known Dropshipping Marketplaces:**

The chapter gives a quick rundown of a few well-known dropshipping websites, emphasising their salient characteristics and intended customer bases:

**Shopify:** Well-liked and approachable, this platform is renowned for its scalability, vast app marketplace, and simplicity of use.

**Woo Commerce:** is a free and open-source platform that offers more freedom and customisation, but it requires more technical know-how to set up and maintain.

**Big Commerce:** An extensive feature set, scalable design for bigger enterprises, and integrated SEO tools characterise this feature-rich platform.

**Spocket:** A dropshipping-focused platform featuring product sourcing tools, order fulfilment automation, and direct supplier connectors.

**1.3. Creating a Successful Dropshipping Website:**

The chapter dives into the crucial components of creating a dropshipping business that converts once you've selected your platform:

**Professional and User-Friendly Design:* Make an investment in a customer-friendly design layout that is neat and well-organised. Make sure your website is mobile-friendly and loads swiftly.

**Excellent Product Photos and Descriptions:** Make use of excellent product photos and captivating product descriptions that effectively highlight the attributes and advantages of your offerings.

**Unambiguous Calls to Action (CTAs):* With calls to action that are obvious and conspicuous, such "Add to Cart" or "Buy Now" buttons, you may help your clients through the purchasing process.

**Reliable Components:** Establish credibility with your clients by showcasing client endorsements, reviews, and easily accessible contact details. Make sure your website has appropriate security measures in place as well.

**Brand Consistency:** To establish a distinctive and memorable brand identity, keep your store's design, branding, and message consistent.

**1.4. Extra Thoughts Into Design:**

The chapter outlines other factors to take into account while designing your dropshipping store:

**Mobile-Friendly Design:** In the mobile-first world of today, making sure your website is responsive to various screen sizes and easily adjusts to them is essential to attracting mobile visitors and generating revenue.

**Search Engine Optimisation (SEO)**: To raise your website's search engine rating and increase the amount of organic traffic it may bring in, apply fundamental SEO best practices to your product pages and content.

**Abandoned basket Recovery:** To reclaim prospective consumers who add products to their basket but quit the transaction, think about putting abandoned cart recovery tactics into practice.

You can build a dropshipping shop that not only looks great but also turns visitors into paying customers, which will greatly increase the success of your dropshipping company. This can be achieved by carefully selecting the proper platform, putting an emphasis on user experience, and putting design best practices into effect.

# Chapter Four

**Developing Your Dropshipping Company: Dropshippers' Marketing and Sales Strategies: Bringing in Clients and Increasing Revenue**

In the cutthroat world of online shopping, a dropshipping company's ability to attract clients and increase revenue is essential. This chapter provides you with practical marketing and sales techniques that can help you create leads, increase brand recognition, and eventually turn website visitors into devoted clients.

****1.1. *Gaining Knowledge of the Marketing Environment:***** The need to comprehend the constantly changing marketing environment is emphasised at the beginning of the chapter. It lists several marketing avenues and strategies, emphasising their advantages and possible uses for dropshipping companies:

***material marketing:*** Producing insightful and useful material, such as blog articles, videos, or social media postings, may draw in new clients, position your company as an industry leader, and raise your website's search engine rating.

**Social Media Marketing:** To engage with your target market, promote your goods, and increase brand recognition, use well-known social media sites like Facebook, Instagram, and TikTok.

**Email Marketing:** Create an email list and run email campaigns to nurture leads, advertise new items, and provide current clients with unique offers.

**Paid Advertising:** To target certain demographics and reach a larger audience, take into consideration paid advertising choices via platforms like Google Ads, Facebook Ads, or Instagram Ads.

**Search Engine Optimisation (SEO):** By incorporating SEO best practices into your website, you may raise its organic search engine position and draw in visitors who are looking for information or items related to your business.

**1.2. Increasing Awareness of Brands:** The chapter stresses the need for creating a brand identity that extends beyond product promotion. Here are various methods to make this happen:

**Create a clear and consistent brand identity:** Ensure that your logo, colour palette, message, and general brand personality are all consistent across all of your marketing platforms.

**Storytelling and Material Creation:** Don't only concentrate on the characteristics of your product; instead, craft captivating tales and provide interesting material that connects with your target audience. This encourages brand loyalty and emotional connection.

**Collaboration and Influencer Marketing:** To increase your reach and get access to well-known personalities' audiences, team up with relevant influencers in your sector or take part in industry gatherings.

**1.3. Successful Dropshipping Sales Techniques:** The chapter delves into certain sales techniques to turn website visitors into paying clients beyond brand awareness:

**High-Quality Photographs and Captivating Product Descriptions:** Make an investment in high-quality product photographs and craft captivating product descriptions that draw attention to the features and advantages of your offerings while addressing any possible issues raised by customers.

**Publishing Calls to Action (CTAs)**: Ensure that your website has obvious and conspicuous calls to action, such as "Add to Cart" or "Buy Now" buttons, to facilitate consumers in taking the intended action.

*__Promotions and Discounts:__* To encourage purchases and instil a feeling of urgency, use well-planned promotions and discounts, such as time-limited deals or seasonal specials.

*__Testimonials and Reviews from Customers:__* Putting up gratifying reviews and testimonials from customers helps increase social proof and trust, which in turn encourages prospective buyers to make a purchase from your shop.

*__Excellent Customer Service:__* Throughout the purchasing process, offering outstanding customer service builds trust and loyalty, promoting recurring business and excellent word-of-mouth referrals.

**_1.4. Examining and Improving Marketing Initiatives:_**The chapter emphasises how crucial it is to monitor and evaluate your marketing initiatives in order to assess their success and make the required modifications for ongoing development. Make use of the analytics tools provided by the platform of your choice or outside services to:

**Track website traffic and conversion rates:* Check where visitors come from and how they use your site to see where you can make improvements.

**Monitor the performance of your marketing campaigns:* examine the efficiency of various marketing channels and modify your tactics to get the most out of them in terms of return on investment (ROI).

**Analysis of customer behaviour:** Learn about the preferences and behaviour of your customers to improve the overall experience of your customers, tailor your marketing messages, and enhance your product offers.

It is possible to draw in prospective clients, turn them into paying customers, and eventually increase revenue for your dropshipping company by combining the marketing and sales techniques covered in this chapter. Remember that in order to remain ahead of the curve in the always-changing world of e-commerce, creating a successful online business needs constant work, data-driven decision-making, and continual optimisation.

# Chapter Five

**Managing and Expanding Your Dropshipping Company:  Crucial  Dropshipping  Resources and Tools: Getting Your Operations in Order**

After laying the groundwork for your dropshipping company, this chapter explores the vital tools and resources that may help you optimise your processes, boost productivity, and eventually free up your time to concentrate on expanding your business.

**1.1. *The Value of Making Use of Tools and Resources:*** The necessity of leveraging technology and making use of the tools and resources that are accessible is emphasised at the beginning of the chapter. These may greatly increase productivity, automate tedious jobs, and free up your important time so you can focus on critical business development strategies for your dropshipping company.

**1.2.Tools for Inventory Management:** Effective inventory management is essential for every dropshipping company. The chapter examines many instruments that may be used to expedite this procedure:

**Inventory Management Software:** With the help of these tools, you can reduce the possibility of overselling or stockouts by tracking stock levels in real-time, receiving low-stock warnings, and synchronising inventory information with your suppliers.

**Order Management Solutions (OMS):** These all-inclusive solutions guarantee a flawless client experience by automating order processing, monitoring order fulfilment, and providing real-time shipment tracking information.

**1.3. *Tools for Marketing and Analytics:*** Success requires both marketing and performance analysis.

***This chapter outlines several important resources to think about such as:***

*Email Marketing Platforms:* Take advantage of intuitive platforms to develop and oversee email campaigns, cultivate leads, and interact with your audience via focused messaging.

*Social Media Management Tools:* With the help of these tools, monitoring consumer interactions, analysing social media activity, and scheduling postings across many platforms are made easier.

*Reporting and Analytics Tools:* Use analytics tools to learn more about consumer behaviour, website traffic, and marketing campaign effectiveness. These insights help you make data-driven choices that will maximise your return on investment (ROI) and optimise your marketing tactics.

## *Tools for Customer Service*

Establishing trust and cultivating loyalty require outstanding customer service. This chapter looks at ways to improve your customer service skills:

A. Live Chat Software: Use live chat features to provide your customers with real-time help so you can quickly and effectively handle their questions.

B. Ticketing Systems: Make use of ticketing systems to effectively handle customer support requests, monitor the status of resolutions, and guarantee that no question is left unanswered.

*Extra Resources and Tools:* In addition to the categories listed above, the chapter delves into further resources that might improve your dropshipping experience.

A. Dropshipping Research Tools: Make use of tools made especially for dropshipping companies to find reputable suppliers, study rivals, and identify popular items.

B. Ecommerce Automation Tools: Free up time for strategic planning and company growth by automating repetitive processes like order processing, social media posting, and email marketing campaigns.

C. Educational Resources: Through online classes, trade journals, and e-commerce groups, keep yourself informed about the latest developments in the dropshipping sector, including best practices, legal issues, and emerging trends.

D. Selecting Appropriate Tools:With so many tools at your disposal, the chapter stresses how important it is to choose the ones that best suit your goals and budget. When assessing and choosing which tools to incorporate into your dropshipping operations, take into account variables such as your business's size, budget, level of technical skill, and required functions.

***Effective Tool Implementation and Utilisation:***It's not enough to just have the correct tools; you also need to use them efficiently. As the text suggests, you should:

**Start with the essentials:** As your company expands, progressively add additional critical tools by starting with a handful that meet your most urgent demands.

**Make an investment in support and training:** Make sure you know how to utilise the selected tools efficiently. Make use of the tutorials, training materials, and customer assistance that the tool providers have available.

** Track and quantify the impact:** Examine how the tools you've introduced are affecting the performance of your company on a regular basis.

This enables you to pinpoint areas in need of development and modify your strategy as needed.You may acquire important insights, automate monotonous work, simplify operations, and free up time to concentrate on the strategic parts of expanding your dropshipping company by using the appropriate tools and resources. To succeed over the long term in the ever-changing world of e-commerce, you will need to continuously learn, adapt, and use technology.

## Managing and Expanding Your Dropshipping Company

A Complete Success GuideAfter covering the essentials and the main features of dropshipping in the preceding chapters, this part explores the continuous process of managing and expanding your dropshipping company. It gives you the know-how and tactics you need to handle day-to-day operations, streamline your workflow, and eventually lead your company to long-term success.

*1.1. Establishing a Long-Term Dropshipping Company:* The first section of the chapter highlights the essential elements that go into creating a successful and long-lasting dropshipping business:

**Pay Attention to Client Satisfaction:** Make delivering first-rate customer care throughout the purchasing process your top priority. This entails communicating with customers promptly, answering their questions effectively, and satisfying their concerns. Recurring business and favourable word-of-mouth referrals depend heavily on developing trust and providing excellent client experiences.

**Ongoing Education and Development:** The world of e-commerce is always changing. Make a commitment to lifelong learning by keeping abreast of regulatory requirements, industry developments, and best practices. Make use of the tools at your disposal, such as online groups, industry journals, and courses, to expand your knowledge and modify your approaches for success.

**Decision Making Based on Data:** Don't depend on your gut feelings alone. Make use of data analytics' potential to learn more about consumer behaviour, website traffic, and the effectiveness of marketing campaigns. To maximise your product offers, marketing plans, and general company operations, make data-driven choices.

**1.2 Dropshippers' Legal and Financial Considerations:** This chapter clarifies important financial and legal factors to take into account while managing your dropshipping business:

**Business Formation and Licencing:** Based on your location and type of business, you may need to register your company and get the necessary licences or permits in order to legally operate.

**Taxes and Regulations:** Recognise your tax responsibilities and make sure that you are in compliance with all applicable laws, including import/export laws if your suppliers are based abroad.

**Financial Management:** Use good financial management techniques, such as keeping thorough books, keeping track of your spending, and keeping an eye on your cash flow, to safeguard the financial stability of your enterprise.

## 1.3. Establishing a Robust Support Network:

Being a successful dropshipper doesn't have to be a one-person show. The chapter advises you to create a network of allies to help you on your journey.

**Networking with other dropshippers:** Use online forums or groups to get in touch with other dropshippers. Create a network of people who share your interests by exchanging experiences and learning from each other's triumphs and setbacks.

**Hiring freelancers or virtual assistants:** As your company grows, think about hiring freelancers or virtual assistants to handle duties like content generation, customer care, and product research to free up your time for business growth and strategic planning.

**8.4. Expanding Your E-Commerce Company:** As your company expands, this chapter offers a road map for effective scaling:

*Expanding Your Product Portfolio:** Give careful thought to introducing new items that enhance your current line of business and meet the changing demands of your intended market.
**Exploring New Markets:** Do some research and think about reaching out to new areas via marketing materials and website translations or partnerships with local fulfilment centres.
**Optimising Your Operations**: Evaluate and improve your operating procedures on a regular

basis. Streamline processes, increase productivity, and free up time to concentrate on key growth objectives by using technology and automation.

***Concluding Remarks:*** The Path of Ongoing Development:In closing, the chapter emphasises that dropshipping is a path of ongoing learning, adaptation, and development, just like any other entrepreneurial endeavour. You may build a strong foundation, overcome obstacles, and successfully traverse the ever-changing world of e-commerce by putting the tactics and best practices described throughout this book into practice. This will help you grow your dropshipping company over time. Recall that perseverance, never-ending education, and the capacity to adjust to the always-changing e-commerce market are the keys to success.

# Chapter six

**Expanding and Increasing Your Dropshipping Company: Long-Term Success Formulas.**

After you've laid the groundwork for your dropshipping company to succeed, this chapter explores long-term tactics for attaining steady development and expanding your organisation. It gives you useful knowledge and strategies to help you through the thrilling but difficult process of growing your company and establishing your name in the e-commerce industry.

1.1. Realising How Important Scaling Is: The necessity of growing your dropshipping company after its first success is emphasised in the first section of the chapter. By scaling, you can:

A. *Boost Sales and Profitability:* Expanding your customer base and maybe increasing your sales volume will help you generate more income and make more money.

B. *Improve Brand Recognition:* Reaching a wider audience will help you become more well-known in your niche by raising brand awareness and recognition.

C. *Optimise Efficiency and Leverage:* You may save costs and enhance overall company performance by scaling your operations and resource utilisation more effectively.

**1.2. Formulating an Expansion Plan:** The need to develop a clear development plan before starting the scaling process is emphasised throughout the chapter. This approach ought to:

A. Define Your Long-Term Vision: Clearly state your drop-shipping company's long-term objectives. What do you expect the next few years to hold for your company?

B. Identify expansion chances: Whether it's growing your product line, pursuing new markets, or investigating other sales methods, there may be chances for expansion that you may uncover with careful market research.

C. Analyse Your Resources: Examine your present resources, such as finances, labour force, and operational capacity, to see if putting your selected development strategy into practice is feasible.

D. Define SMART objectives: For your development plan, use the SMART framework to define objectives that are precise, quantifiable, realistic, pertinent, and time-bound. This guarantees your scaling initiatives have direction and clarity.

**1.3. Essential Techniques for Growing Your Dropshipping Company:** The chapter delves into certain tactics you might use to scale successfully:

A. Building Your Product Portfolio: Gradually add new items to your line-up that enhance what you already have and address the changing demands and preferences of your target market. Strike a balance between launching new items and making sure your current product line is profitable and of the highest calibre.

B. Exploring other markets: Do some research and think about reaching out to other areas. To efficiently serve clients from abroad, this might include translating your website and marketing materials or collaborating with local fulfilment facilities.

C. Optimising Your Marketing Efforts: Make constant improvements to your marketing tactics in order to expand your audience and draw in new clients. Make use of data analytics to determine which marketing channels are most successful for your company and modify your budget appropriately.

D. Building Brand Loyalty: To promote repeat business and favourable word-of-mouth referrals, cultivate strong customer connections by delivering great customer service, introducing loyalty programmes, and putting customised marketing tactics into practice.

E. Leveraging Technology and Automation: Make use of automation and technological tools to increase productivity, optimise processes, and free up time for strategic growth projects. This might include putting chatbots for customer support, automated marketing tools, or inventory management technologies into use.

F. Forming Strategic Partnerships: Take into account collaborating with companies in related sectors or in your area of expertise. To increase your reach and clientele, this may include working together on marketing initiatives, looking into cross-promotional possibilities, or investigating dropshipping agreements with other companies.

G.  Putting Money Into Your Brand: As your company grows, make an investment in creating a distinctive and powerful brand identity. This entails creating a unified brand voice, purchasing premium branding supplies, and setting up a credible web presence.

**1.4. Obstacles in Scaling and Ways to Get Past Them:** The chapter addresses some of the many difficulties that might occur during scaling, including:

A. Managing Increased Inventory Complexity: To keep track of stock levels, maintain product quality, and prevent stockouts, expanding your product variety calls for effective inventory management solutions.

B. Maintaining Customer Service Quality: As your clientele expands, it becomes more important to maintain a high standard of customer care across all interactions.To manage typical questions, think about growing your customer support staff or introducing self-service solutions like FAQs or chatbots.

C. Marketing and Reaching a Wider Audience: Enhanced marketing methods and maybe higher marketing expenditures are needed to successfully reach a wider audience and draw in new clients.

D. Maintaining Operational Efficiency: It's critical to keep operations running smoothly as your company grows. This entails monitoring your operations on a regular basis, spotting bottlenecks, and automating as much as you can.

## 1.5. Final Thoughts: The Path to Prolonged Achievement:

The last point made in the chapter is that growing your dropshipping company is an ongoing process that calls for commitment, flexibility, and a readiness to change and grow. You can successfully manage the hurdles of growing and create a path for long-term success in the dynamic world of e-commerce by putting the tactics described in this book into practice, keeping an eye on your progress, and making adjustments based on consumer feedback and market trends.

Bonus

## Case Studies on Dropshipping: Gaining Knowledge from Prosperous Enterprises

An appreciation of the experiences of successful dropshipping companies may provide prospective company owners with insightful knowledge and motivation. By dissecting their tactics, accomplishments, and even setbacks, you may learn a great deal and create a plan for your own dropshipping business.

Here are several instances of successful dropshipping companies, along with some important lessons learned from their experiences:

**1. CloudSharks:** Shark-shaped slippers are the product.

Success factors:

**Unique product:** made money by capitalising on a product that was in great demand and had little competition.* **Powerful social media marketing:** Reached a wide audience by using platforms like Facebook Ads, Instagram marketing, and TikTok marketing.

**Resonant brand identity:** Created a distinctive brand voice and image that connected with their target market.

## 2. Bullet with Fruit:

**Product:** a little fruit blender

Success Factors: made use of TikTok's viral marketing capabilities to get early momentum and general notice.

**Mobile-friendly website:** Guaranteed a smooth user experience for consumers browsing and shopping on mobile devices.

**Targeted marketing:** Concentrated marketing efforts on platforms frequented by their target audience, such as young adults and health enthusiasts.

3. Product: Sustainable kitchen and homeware items * Success factors:

** Niche focus: **Designed to appeal to a certain market that is becoming more and more interested in eco-friendly goods. **Exceptional

product assortment:** placed a premium on ethical sourcing and quality, fostering a relationship of trust with their clientele.
**Marketing content:** authored interesting and educational blog entries and social media posts on sustainability, drawing in natural traffic and instructing their audience.

**Important Lessons from These Case Studies**

Identifying a niche: Especially for new dropshipping companies in a crowded industry, focusing on a specialised clientele with certain demands or interests may be a profitable approach.

Leveraging social media marketing: Reaching a large audience and increasing brand recognition may be accomplished by making great use of social media sites like Facebook, Instagram, and TikTok.

Creating a powerful brand identity: Differentiating your brand from the competition and connecting with your target market are made possible by developing a distinctive brand image and voice.

Putting the customer experience front and centre: Establishing trust and encouraging customer loyalty requires offering premium items, first-rate customer service, and an easy-to-use website.

Flexibility and ongoing education: The world of e-commerce is always changing. Long-term success requires being flexible in the face of trends, taking note of successful companies' practices, and doing your own data analysis.These are just a few of the several dropshipping companies that have found success using different tactics and methods. Through examining their narratives, pinpointing applicable insights, and incorporating them into your own business strategy, you may enhance your prospects of triumphing in the fascinating and ever-changing realm of dropshipping.